Tweens and Teens

A Cookbook to Get You Started

Nancy N Wilson

Tweens and Teens

A Cookbook to Get You Started

Published June 2019
United States of America

ISBN: 978-1-7330941-1-5

Title Page Image by Paleka through ShutterStock

Dedication

To young people everywhere who want to learn how to cook and have fun in the kitchen!

A special dedication to my five beautiful granddaughters, Eve, Kaitlin, Miranda, Charlotte, and Bella

Thank You

... for buying my book.
If you enjoy it, please take a minute and
post a review on Amazon and Goodreads or
any other platform where you purchased the book.

For a complete list of Nancy N Wilson's published cookbooks,
please, visit my Websites
https://MamasLegacyCookcooks.com
https://NancyNWilson.com

Nancy N. Wilson

Please help improve my book.
If you find errors or omissions, or have a problem with a recipe,
please, contact Nancy N Wilson immediately at: wilsonemarketing@gmail.com,
so corrections can be made.

Table of Contents

Introduction

Welcome to the world of cooking – it is a wonderful adventure that should be enjoyed by everyone!

When my granddaughter was only four years old, she wanted to learn how to cook. In the beginning, I would put ingredients in a bowl and she would stir. Then, she learned to break eggs into a dish so I could scramble them, while she made the toast.

Then, little by little she learned how to measure flour and sugar, how to cut cherry tomatoes and cucumbers, how to mix things with the electric mixer, how to turn on the oven, set the timer, and so on.

As soon as she learned to read, we would practice reading recipes. She would read the recipe to (step-by-step). I would let her do what she could and I would do the rest.

She is now almost 11, and can do most of the work, with my supervision. I'm always nearby in case she needs help.

She can make a cake, pumpkin pie (except for the crust), and cookies by herself (except putting pans in and taking them out of the oven, which is still difficult to do without spilling the batter or burning herself.)

She can scramble eggs, make salads, and lots of other things with practically no supervision, but I remain close to lend a hand when necessary.

Everyone should learn to cook! It is a fun, creative, activity. It is also very satisfying when young people can prepare and serve their families a tasty dish that they've made. One of the best things is that their friends will be in awe of the fact that someone their age can cook!

The book contains a list of ***essential tools*** that will make the cooking process much easier.

There is also a ***list of safety tips,*** which will make them "smart" cooks and keep them safe in the kitchen.

There is a nice variety of recipes that my granddaughter has mastered over the past six years; plus, a few that are newer and more challenging.

There are easy, healthy choices for breakfast, lunch and dinner – and, of course, sweets and desserts.

If you are young or completely inexperienced, we recommend that you always have supervision to keep you safe and to help you over the rough spots.

If you are a little older and have been cooking for a while, you can probably cook mostly on your own; but, it is wise to have an adult in the house with you for safety reasons.

It is time to ***have fun in your kitchen*** and learn how to cook – a skill that will serve you well your entire life!

I hope you enjoy cooking as much my granddaughter does.

Nancy

Essential Tools

Set of Mixing Bowls	Measuring Cups & Spoons	Liquid Measuring Cups

Pyrex Glass Mixing Bowl Set	U-Taste 10 Piece Measuring Cups and Spoons Set	Anchor 77940 3-Piece Measuring Cup Set
Wooden Cutting Board	Handheld Electric Mixer	Set of Wooden Spoons
	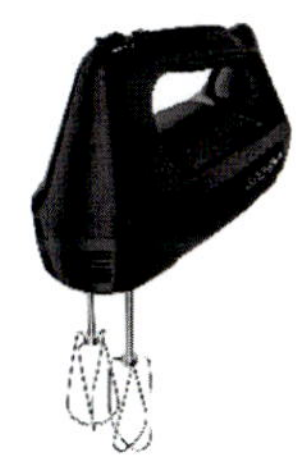	
Organic Bamboo Cutting Board with Juice Groove - Anti Microbial	BLACK+DECKER 6-Speed Hand Mixer	Wooden Spoons Set for Cooking
Wire Whisk	Rubber Spatula	Pancake Turner
	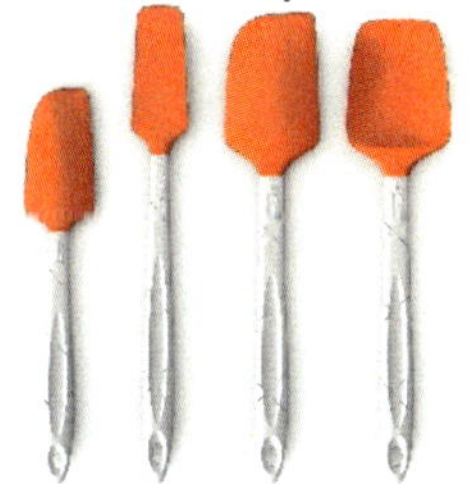	
OXO Good Grips 11-Inch Better Balloon Whisk	Heat Resistant Silicone Spatulas Set	Dexter-Russell Pancake Turner, Stainless Steel with Walnut Handle

Sharp Cutting Knives	Chef Knives	Vegetable Peeler
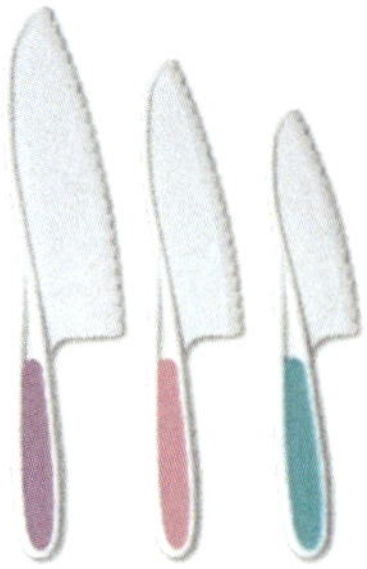 Tovla Children's Cooking Knives	 Mercer Culinary Renaissance 6-Piece Forged Knife Block Set	 OXO 20081 Peeler, Swivel, Black
Dutch Oven  Lodge 6 Quart Enameled Cast Iron Dutch Oven	Small (1-egg) Frying Pan  GreenPan Mini Ceramic Non-Stick Round Egg Pan	Griddle  Farberware Nonstick Aluminum 11-Inch Square Griddle
Cast Iron Frying Pan  Pre-seasoned 12" Cast Iron Skillet - Red Silicone Hot Handle Holder	Spring-form Pan  9-inch Springform Baking Pan	9 X 13 Baking Pan  Pyrex Glass Oblong Baking Dish

8-Inch Square Baking Pan  Pyrex Basics 8-inch Square	Cookie Sheets (2)  Non-Stick Mega Large Cookie Pan	9-inch Pie Plate  Pyrex Glass Bakeware Pie Plate 9" x 1.2" Pack of 2
6-Well Muffin Pan  Wilton Non-Stick 6-Cup Standard Muffin Pan, 2 Pack	12-Well Muffin Pan 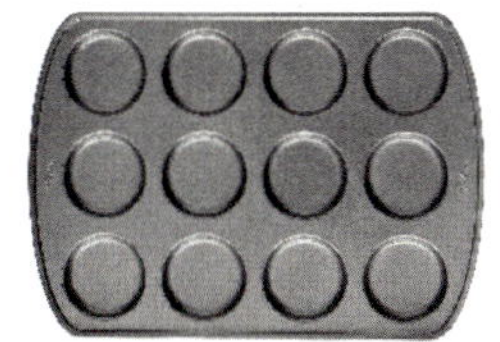 Wilton Non-Stick Muffin Baking Pan, 12-Cup	Mini-Muffin Pan 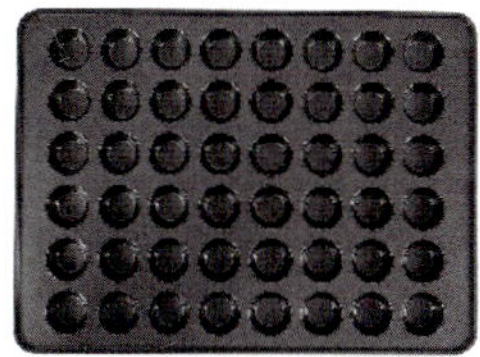 Non-Stick, 48-Cup Mega Mini-Muffin Pan
Cookie Scoops  Norpro Stainless Steel Cookie Scoops, Set of 3	Pastry Wheel Cutter  Double Pastry Wheel	Microwave Cooking Plate  Bacon Grlll wlth Vented Cover

Jelly Roll Pan	Garlic Press	Pie Crust Edge Protector
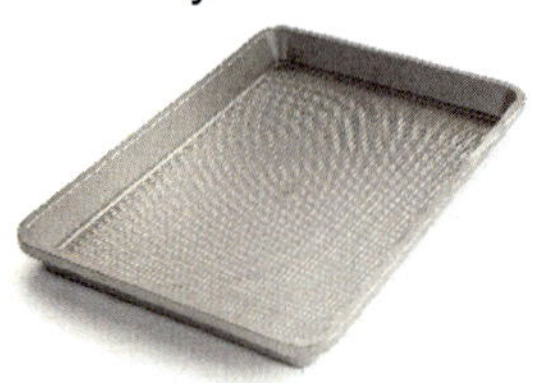		
Non-Stick Pro Jelly Roll 10 x 15 Inch	Soft-Handled Garlic Press	Pie Crust Protector Shield for 9-inch Pies

Kitchen Safety Tips for Young Cooks

Since my granddaughter and I started cooking together when she was only four, I wanted to be very clear that learning how to be safe in the kitchen was the most important lesson of all.

Even though she knew the rules, she would sometimes forget and I would have to gently reminds her, so that she would be safe.

Knowing and following the rules not only keeps her safe, it also teaches her how to be control of the cooking process. When she stays within the guidelines, she knows what she is doing at all times and has better results.

If you are a younger tween, read through the rules carefully, review them with your favorite adult cook, and add any rules you think are important that we may have missed.

If you are older and allowed to cook unsupervised, please, read the rules regularly so that they are locked in your mind and will keep you safe while you are in the kitchen.

My granddaughter and I put together the following list of safety tips for you. Read them carefully before you start.

HAVE FUN AND BE SAFE!

Safety Tips

Always Ask Permission Before Starting to Cook

For very young or inexperienced cooks it is important to always have an adult with you, or nearby, when you are cooking.

Dress Smart for Cooking

a. **An apron is recommended.**

b. **It is best to wear clean, snug clothes with tight, short sleeves – nothing loose and dangling that can catch fire.**

c. **When first learning to cook, wear older clothes because there will be spills and splashes that manage to hit areas not covered by the apron.**

d. **Keep longer hair securely tied back so you don't get hair in your food and there is no danger of it catching on fire.**

Always Work with Clean, Dry Hands

a. Clean, dry hands are critical in food safety.

b. Washing your hands is always the first step before touching any food or appliance . . . and wash again, as needed, during the cooking process. Unwanted germs in the food you are preparing can make people sick.

c. Wash your hands with soap after handling raw meat – especially chicken.

d. Rinse your hands as necessary to keep them clean and dry – wet hands can be slippery.

Keep a Clean, Tidy Kitchen

a. ***Clean as you go*** by wiping counters and cleaning up spills when they happen. This keeps the area sanitary, non-slippery, and clear so you have plenty of space to work.

b. Put ingredients away as soon as you are finished with them.

c. Steps (a) and (b) above make the kitchen cleanup much quicker when you are finished cooking.

d. Close cabinet doors and drawers completely so you don't bump into them and hurt yourself.

Learn to Use Appliances Correctly

a. Have someone teach you how to use the oven, stovetop, and microwave correctly.

b. Be sure the stove top is clear before turning on a burner.

c. Check electrical cords on portable appliances to be sure they are in good condition (no breaks or frayed cords).

d. Keep all portable electrical appliances away from water so you don't get shocked.

e. Keep electrical cords away from the stove top, oven, and sink.

f. Don't plug in an appliance with wet hands.

g. When you have finished cooking, before you leave the kitchen, be sure that small appliances are stored properly and the oven and stove-top burners are turned off.

Protect Yourself from Burns

a. It is easy to get burned in the kitchen, so it is critical to know how to avoid burns and to know what to do if it happens.

b. Never cook with dangling sleeves, loose clothing, or loose long hair that can catch on fire. This is even more important when cooking on a gas stovetop.

c. When using the oven, pay attention to all parts of the oven so you do not accidentally burn yourself as you put pans in or take them out of the oven.

d. Always use hot pads/potholders when handling and carrying hot pans and when removing pans from the oven and microwave.

e. Never add water to a pan that has hot oil in it. The oil will splatter and burn anyone nearby.

f. If you burn yourself, alert the supervising adult immediately, and put the burned area under cold running water.

g. When stirring something in a pot on the stove top, be sure to hold the handle with your non-dominant hand to prevent the pot from slipping off the burner and spilling on you or someone else.

h. When letting something simmer on the stove top, always turn pot handles toward the back of the stove so that no one can bump into them and knock over the pot.

Manage the Risk of Fire

a. Keep paper towels, dish towels, and pot holders away from the range top so they don't catch on fire.

b. If a fire starts, get help quickly!

c. Have a fire extinguisher in the kitchen and know how to use it.

d. Never use water on a kitchen fire, it may make the fire bigger.

e. A small fire can be put out with baking soda or smothered with a lid.

f. If the fire turns into leaping flames, leave the house and call 911 immediately.

Learn How to Use Knives Correctly

1. Watch where and how you are cutting.
2. Never cut toward your body or your hand. Always cut away from your fingers and body.
3. Don't put knives or other sharp objects in a sink full of water.
4. If you are young or inexperienced, never cut anything without supervision.
5. Always use sharp knives - a sharp, **clean knife** is a **safe knife**.
6. Store knives in a knife block.
7. Hold sharp knives correctly

    a. **Pinch Grip** - Professional chefs will almost always promote holding a knife with a pinch grip where the thumb and forefinger pinch the bottom of the blade. It allows for control and steadies the hand when cutting.

    b. **Pointer Grip** - Place an index finger along the top of the knife, which will steady your hand. This is usually easier for smaller hands. The important thing is to have good control of the knife and to be safe.

Use the technique that is the most comfortable. I suggest practicing both techniques and see which feels the most natural to you.

8. Learn How to Cut Safely

Always use a common safety technique called, ***the claw***.

It is very simple and natural. For example, you hold a tomato with your non-dominant hand by curling your hand into a claw-like shape, with your fingernails holding the food. Keep your hand in this position to stabilize the food and away from the knife as you cut, which limits the risk of a serious injury.

9. Stand Up Straight

    a. This will keep you balanced, alert, and focused while using a knife or any other cutting tool.

10. Practice safe cutting techniques with fruits and vegetables like bananas, cucumbers and peppers. Start with starter knives and graduate to real cooking knives.

Handle Food Properly

a. Always work with clean hands.

b. Always use clean plates and utensils.

c. Never put fresh vegetables or cooked food on an unwashed plate or cutting board that has held uncooked meat.

d. Always cut meat and chicken on a cutting board and wash thoroughly with soap when you are finished.

After you have carefully reviewed the above rules, discuss them with your mom or another adult cooking friend and add rules they have, which can be useful – and will keep you safe.

BREAKFAST

Avocado Toast

Recipe makes 1 serving

Avocado toast is creamy, crisp and delicious. It is a quick, easy, healthy breakfast, or yummy snack! It is best to eat anything with avocado right away because it begins to turn brown quickly.

INGREDIENTS

- 1 thick slice of your favorite bread
- ½ ripe avocado
- Salt and pepper
- Extra toppings of your choice (optional)

EXTRA TOPPPINGS

- Sliced cherry tomatoes
- Finely chopped onions and/or salsa
- Fried, scrambled or poached egg

DIRECTIONS

1. Cut the avocado in half and remove the pit.
2. Carefully scoop the avocado from the peeling into a small bowl.
3. Mash it with a fork until it is smooth (you can leave small chunks if you like).
4. Add a little salt (about ⅛ teaspoon) – start with a little and add more to taste.
5. Toast the bread the way you like it.
6. Spread avocado on top of your toast.
7. Sprinkle lightly with pepper (optional).
8. Enjoy every bite with just the avocado – or add extra toppings.

Banana Egg Pancakes

Recipe makes 1 serving of four 5-inch pancakes

These delicious pancakes are filled with healthy goodness. Yummy when sprinkled with powdered sugar or topped with butter and honey or pure maple syrup.

INGREDIENTS

- 1 ripe banana mashed
- 1 cage free egg
- 2 tablespoons half and half (or milk)
- ¼ cup pancake flour
- Dash of salt

DIRECTIONS

1. In small mixing bowl mash banana until very soft.
2. Add egg and milk.
3. Beat with a fork or wire whisk until fluffy.

4. Add pancake flour and dash of salt.
5. Beat again until flour is mixed in completely.
6. Heat griddle until medium hot.
7. Coat griddle lightly with butter.
8. Pour small amounts of batter onto griddle – makes four pancakes. *(Or cook as one large pancake on the griddle or in a small round frying pan. This is also delicious but a little more difficult to flip.)*
9. Cook on first side until bubbles start to form and edges are cooked.
10. Flip the pancake and continue cooking until second side is lightly browned.
11. Lower the heat, if necessary, to prevent burning.

Ham and Egg Birds Nest

Recipe makes 6 servings

This is a fun and healthy breakfast that you can cook for the family. They will love it. Add hot buttered toast and a dish of strawberries for a complete meal.

INGREDIENTS

- Softened butter (to grease the muffin cups)
- 6 thin slices of ham
- 6 cage-free eggs
- 6 teaspoons salsa (optional)
- ¾ cup grated cheese (Colby-Jack, Cheddar, or Parmesan)
- 3 finely-sliced green onions
- Salt and pepper, to taste

DIRECTIONS

1. Preheat oven to 350° F.
2. Grate the cheese and chop the onions.

3. Lightly grease each muffin cup with butter.
4. Line each muffin cup with a ham slice, so that it creates a nice nest for the egg.
5. Bake at 350°F for 5 minutes.
6. Remove the pan from the oven and crack one egg into each cup.
7. Salt and pepper, to taste.
8. Top with salsa, grated cheese, and sliced green onions.
9. Return to oven and bake for 12 minutes more.
10. Check doneness of eggs – if OK, remove from oven. If not, continue to bake for one minute at a time until done to your liking.
11. Slip each nest onto a plate and serve.

NOTE: If you do not like spicy foods, don't use the salsa.

Healthy Crunchy Granola

Recipe makes 6 cups

This is a healthy easy-to-make, gluten-free granola filled with spice and nuts. It is tasty for breakfast as cereal with milk or yogurt, or for eating alone as a snack.

INGREDIENTS

- 3 cups quick or old-fashioned oats
- 1 cup chopped pecans (almonds/walnuts/pine nuts)
- 1 cup pepitas (shelled pumpkin seeds)
- ¼ cup wheat germ
- ½ cup dried cherries or cranberries
- 1 teaspoon ground cinnamon
- ½ teaspoon salt
- 1/8 teaspoon ground cloves
- 1/8 teaspoon nutmeg
- 1 teaspoon vanilla extract
- 1/3 cup organic honey
- ¼ cup oil (melted coconut or canola)

DIRECTIONS

1. Preheat oven to 350°F.
2. Place a silicone baking mat or parchment paper on large cookie sheet and set aside.
3. Place all ingredients _except the dried cranberries or cherries_ in a large bowl – dry ingredients first.
4. Mix lightly until the dry ingredients are well coated with the wet ingredients (vanilla, honey, and oil).
5. Spread mixture evenly onto prepared baking sheet.
6. Bake in preheated oven for 30 minutes (stir carefully after 15 minutes).
7. Remove from oven and stir in the dried cranberries or cherries – be sure to mix thoroughly.
8. Cool completely and store in an airtight container in pantry for up to two weeks or in the freezer for up to two months.

Microwave Bacon

Recipe makes 2 servings (2 slices each)

This is an easy, safe way for kids to cook bacon for themselves. It typically takes 1 minute per strip of bacon to cook well (not crispy).

NOTE: The cooking time can vary, so watch the bacon carefully so it doesn't get too crispy.

INGREDIENTS

- 4 slices naturally cured bacon (no nitrates)

DIRECTIONS

1. Layout slices side-by-side on cooking plate – or on clean, doubled paper towels.
2. Cover with lid or a clean paper towel.
3. Microwave on high for 2 minutes – check for doneness.
4. Microwave 30 seconds to 1 minute longer until done to taste.
5. Serve at once.

Overnight Oatmeal

Recipe serves 1 – you can make 2 servings simply by doubling the amount of each ingredient

Try this easy, protein-packed, healthy, delicious breakfast that most kids can make by themselves at night and have it ready in the morning to enjoy before rushing off to school.

INGREDIENTS

- ⅓ cup oats
- Dash of salt
- ⅓ cup whole milk or half-and-half
- ⅓ cup plain Greek yogurt
- 1 or 2 teaspoons organic honey
- 1 tablespoon chia seeds or wheat germ (optional)
- Large dash of cinnamon (optional)

Extras you can add for flavor and fun:

- Diced bananas or strawberries
- Sliced grapes
- Whole blueberries
- Chopped nuts (sliced almonds, pecans, and walnuts are good)
- Heaping teaspoon peanut or almond butter

DIRECTIONS

1. Place all the ingredients (except extras: fruit/nuts/etc.) in a cereal bowl or pint jar.
2. Stir well until mixture is completely blended and smooth.
3. Cover with foil or lid, and place in the fridge until morning.
4. When ready to have breakfast, add the extras (fruit/nuts/etc.), a little more milk, stir well and enjoy every bite.
5. Bacon slices are a very tasty side dish.

Gramme's Scrambled Eggs with Cheese

Recipe serves 1 – double the ingredients if you need 2 servings

This is one of the first things I learned to cook with Gramme, and one of my favorite breakfasts. Try them, you will love them.

AND . . . you can whip them up all by yourself with only a little supervision

TOOLS

Small Frying Pan

Small mixing bowl

Wire whisk

Wooden Spoon

INGREDIENTS

- 1 teaspoon butter
- 2 fresh cage-free eggs
- 1 tablespoon half-and-half
- Salt and Pepper
- 1 or 2 heaping tablespoons shredded cheese

DIRECTIONS

1. Set the shredded cheese where you can reach it easily.
2. Crack eggs into small mixing bowl.
3. Add half-and-half (or milk).
4. Beat with wire whisk until eggs are fluffy.
5. Sprinkle with a little salt and pepper.
6. Place frying pan on stove over medium heat.
7. When pan is hot, spread the butter evenly over the bottom of the pan.
8. Pour the egg mixture into the pan.
9. Stir continuously with wooden spoon (be sure to go around the edges and across the bottom of the pan so it stays evenly scrambled).
10. When eggs are cooked the way you like them, remove the pan from the stove, add cheese and gently fold into the eggs.
11. Scrape the eggs onto your serving plate and breakfast is ready.
12. Buttered toast and jam - with (or without bacon) - goes great with the eggs.

LUNCH AND DINNER

Best Grilled Cheese Sandwich

Recipe makes one sandwich

The secret ingredient in this sandwich is the mayonnaise. Don't be afraid to use it. Once you do, you will never make another grilled cheese without it.

Tools

Griddle or heavy frying pan
Pancake turner
Saucer
Sharp knife

INGREDIENTS

- 2 slices of your favorite fresh bread, (whole wheat, sour dough or rich white bread) Each slice should not be more than ½ inch thick
- 2 teaspoons butter (not margarine)

- 1 tablespoon Hellmann's® or Best Foods® Real Mayonnaise
- 1 to 2 slices real Cheddar Cheese (Tillamook, Colby Jack, or Monterey Jack)

DIRECTIONS

1. Heat a **heavy** frying pan or griddle over medium-low heat.
2. Spread mayonnaise on one side of each slice of bread.
3. Place the cheese slices on the mayo on one slice of bread and top with the 2nd slice of bread – mayo face down on the cheese.
4. Generously butter the top slice of bread and place carefully in the heated pan with the buttered side down. Place a saucer on top of the sandwich.
5. Adjust the heat so the bread sizzles gently; but, doesn't burn.
6. When the cheese looks like it is getting soft, remove the saucer and butter the top slice of bread.
7. Use a spatula to flip the sandwich over so the freshly buttered slice is now on the bottom.
8. Turn the heat down a little more and press firmly to compact the sandwich.
9. After a minute or two, turn the sandwich over several times, pressing gently after each turn, until the sandwich is compact, both sides are crusty, and the cheese is melted (beginning to squish out of the sides.
10. Place the sandwich on a plate, cut in half with a sharp knife, and enjoy.

Chicken and Cheese Quesadillas

Recipe serves 1 or 2 – depending on how much you eat

Most people enjoy this Mexican-style dish, but it is a bit more complicated to prepare than some of the other recipes. You will need supervision for this recipe until you are a little older or have prepared it several times.

TOOLS

Sharp knife

Cutting board

Onion chopper (optional)

Small bowls for the ingredients

Griddle

Serving dishes

INGREDIENTS

- 2 teaspoons very soft butter
- 4 flour tortillas (8-inch)

- 1 cup shredded cheddar cheese
- 1/3 cup finely-diced onion
- 1 large roasted chicken breast – cut in very small cubes

DIRECTIONS

1. Place the soft butter in a small dish close to the stove.
2. Prepare the cheese, onions, and chicken and set those close to the stove also.
3. Place griddle on the stove over medium heat.
4. Lay tortillas on clean, dry paper towels and spread soft butter all over one side of each tortilla.
5. Place two tortillas on the hot griddle (buttered-side down) and sprinkle each with ½ of the cheese, onion, and chicken.
6. Top with the two remaining tortillas, buttered-side up.
7. Cook over medium heat for 3-4 minutes on the first side (until lightly browned and cheese has begun to melt); and then turn. *(You may need help with the turning, it can be tricky.)*
8. Cook on the second side until it is also lightly browned.
9. Remove from heat and cut into wedges.
10. Serve with Fruit Salad or Green Salad. YUMMY!

Deviled Eggs

Recipe makes 6 servings (2 halves each serving)

This is a very old family recipe that I hope you will enjoy. It will take supervision the first few times, for the boiling of the eggs and the slicing into halves, but you will get very good at it quickly.

TOOLS

Large pan with tight-fitting lid

Sharp knife

Cutting board

Large platter

Medium mixing bowl

Large table fork

Large tablespoon

INGREDIENTS

- 2 teaspoons softened real butter
- 6 large cage-free eggs
- 2 tablespoons Hellman's® or Best Foods® Mayonnaise

- 1 teaspoon yellow mustard
- 1 teaspoon Dijon mustard
- 2 teaspoon sweet gherkin pickle juice
- ½ teaspoon sugar
- Large dash of salt and pepper
- Dash of Tabasco Sauce (if you like it a little spicy)
- Paprika

DIRECTIONS

1. Measure and set out the butter so it can soften.
2. Hard Boil the eggs *(needs supervision).*
   a. Place eggs in saucepan and cover completely with water.
   b. Set on stove top over high heat.
   c. Let water come to a full boil and boil for one minute.
   d. Cover with a tight lid and remove from heat.
   e. Let eggs sit in hot water for a FULL 17 minutes.
   f. Drain completely and cover with water and lots of ice.
   g. Let them sit in the ice bath until completely cool – then peel, place on a platter, cover with a light cloth or paper towel; set aside until ready to make deviled eggs.
   NOTE: if more than ½ hour, place eggs in the refrigerator.
3. With a sharp knife, carefully slice the eggs in half (the long way), *which will need supervision.*
4. Carefully remove each yolk from the white and place them in a medium bowl.
5. Set the egg white halves carefully back on the platter.
6. Mash the yolks with a fork.
7. Add mayonnaise, very soft butter, both mustards, pickle juice, sugar, salt, pepper, and Tabasco Sauce.

8. Mix everything together with a fork.
9. Gently spoon the mixture into each egg white – forming a little mound.
10. Sprinkle with paprika.
11. If you love pickles, you can top each egg with a small chunk of sweet gherkin pickle.
12. These eggs make the perfect side dish to serve at a picnic, as an extra dish for dinner, or to eat as a healthy snack.

Fresh Fruit Salad

Recipe makes 4 servings

There is nothing quite as good as fresh ripe fruit, especially a combination of all the best pieces – like the ones we selected. Serve the salad plain (fruit only), with the secret ingredient (dry pudding mix) added, or with *Crème Fraiche* or lightly-sweetened whipped cream as toppings.

INGREDIENTS

- 1 pound of strawberries, stems removed and quartered
- 1 cup blueberries
- 1 cup raspberries
- 2 white peaches, or nectarines, peeled and sliced
- ½ small fresh pineapple, peeled/cored/cubed
- 1 cup seedless grapes (black, red, or green)

- 2 tablespoons vanilla instant pudding mix – use the dry powder
- A few fresh mint leaves for garnish

NOTE: Experiment with other fruits and find the combination you like the best. The fruits listed in this recipe are my favorites – what will yours be?

DIRECTIONS

1. Prepare the fruit as noted above (always use organic, if possible).
2. Be sure to rinse the fruit well, especially the berries and grapes.
3. Dry off any excess water with a clean paper towel and place all the fruit in a large glass bowl.
4. Add the secret ingredient: the dry vanilla pudding mix (optional)
5. Gently toss the fruit until all pieces are covered.
6. Place the bowl in the refrigerator until ready to serve.
7. Before serving, stir carefully and sprinkle a few fresh mint leaves on the top.

Green Salad

Recipe makes 4 servings

This simple salad goes well with almost any meal – especially grilled steak, roasted chicken, or spaghetti and meatballs.

INGREDIENTS for SALAD

- ½ small head of iceberg lettuce, shredded
- 3 or 4 leaves of romaine lettuce, shredded
- 20 cherry tomatoes, washed well and cut in half
- 2 baby cucumbers, washed well, ends removed and sliced very thin
- 1 whole avocado (optional), peeling and pit removed
- Small bunch of fresh dill (optional), minced

INGREDIENTS for DRESSING

- 2 cloves garlic, crushed
- 4 tablespoons of sour cream
- 3 tablespoons of Hellman's® or Best Foods® Mayonnaise
- Salt and freshly-ground pepper to taste

DIRECTIONS

Make the Salad

1. Rinse vegetables very carefully – be sure they are well drained and dry before preparing for the salad.
2. Shred iceberg lettuce by cutting head in half and then, slice each half into ½ inch slices, and finally, chop into smaller pieces.
3. Place shredded lettuce in large salad bowl.
4. Romaine lettuce: Rinse thoroughly, dry with paper towel and break into bite-sized pieces on top of the iceberg lettuce.
5. Baby Cucumbers: Remove most of the dark peeling and trim both ends. Then, slice into round thin slices on top of the lettuce.
6. Cherry tomatoes: Carefully cut in half and place on top of the cucumbers.
7. Avocado: Cut in half and remove pit. Peel carefully and cut into medium small chunks on top of the tomatoes.
8. Finely chop the fresh dill if you are using it and sprinkle into the bowl.
9. Gently toss all ingredients until well-mixed.

Make the Dressing

1. Measure and scoop the sour cream into a small bowl.
2. Add the mayonnaise.
3. Peel and crush the garlic with a garlic press and add to bowl.
4. Add salt and freshly-ground black pepper, to taste.
5. Mix until all ingredients are well-blended.

NOTE: You can serve the salad plain as shown in the picture with dressing on the side so people can add the amount they prefer – or before you serve the salad, you can pour the dressing over the salad and toss it gently until all the ingredients are well-covered.

Guacamole

Recipe makes 4 servings

Gramme grew up in Arizona and loves Mexican food. It is also a favorite of mine. Guacamole is not only easy to prepare and delicious, it is a healthy dish. It is perfect for a snack or as the first part of a Mexican dinner.

INGREDIENTS

- 2 large (about 8 oz) ripe avocados, peeled and seed removed
- 1½ limes, juice only
- 1 medium tomato, washed, ends removed, and finely diced
- ½ medium white onion, chopped very fine
- 1/8 teaspoon freshly ground pepper
- ¼ teaspoon salt

- 1 large clove garlic, minced
- Large dash cumin
- Large dash cayenne pepper
- Pinch of sugar
- 1/3 bunch fresh cilantro, finely chopped without stems
- ½ serrano chili (optional), finely chopped

DIRECTIONS

1. Place peeled and pitted avocados in a large flat bowl.
2. Mash with a fork – OK to leave a few small chunks.
3. Mix in all remaining ingredients.
4. Serve immediately with plenty of fresh tortilla chips.

Easy Macaroni and Cheese

Recipe makes 6 servings

Mac and Cheese always makes you feel warm and cozy. This recipe is easy to make and scrumptious to eat. For young and inexperienced cooks, this one requires supervision.

INGREDIENTS

- 16 ounces uncooked elbow macaroni
- ¼ cup butter (½ stick)
- ¼ cup flour
- ½ teaspoon salt
- 1 dash freshly ground pepper
- 2 cups milk (or 1 cup milk and 1 cup half & half)
- 2 cups shredded cheddar cheese (8 oz package shredded cheddar cheese)

DIRECTIONS

1. Cook macaroni according to package directions in a large pan of salted boiling water – cook to al dente or a little longer, if you prefer.

While macaroni is cooking . . . Make the sauce

2. In medium saucepan, melt butter over medium heat.
3. Sprinkle flour into the butter and cook for 3-5 minutes, stirring constantly with a wire whisk.
4. Add salt and pepper.
5. Slowly add milk, stirring with whisk after each addition.
6. Cook and stir until bubbly.

7. Add a small amount of cheese at a time, continuously stirring until cheese is fully melted.
8. Remove from heat if macaroni is not ready.
9. Drain macaroni, drizzle one teaspoon olive oil on top, and stir. This will keep the macaroni from sticking together.
10. Pour macaroni into hot cheese sauce; stir until all macaroni is well-coated.
11. Do a taste test and add a little more salt and pepper, if needed.
12. Serve immediately with steamed, lighted-buttered broccoli – YUM!

Healthy Macaroni Salad

Recipe makes 6 servings

This easy-to-make salad is tasty all by itself. It is also an excellent choice to serve with hamburgers or hot dogs at a picnic, a summer barbeque, or on camping trips.

INGREDIENTS

- 1 cup dry elbow macaroni
- 4 cups water
- Lemon juice from ½ lemon
- 2 hard-boiled, cage-free eggs, diced
- ½ cup grated cheddar cheese (or feta cheese)
- ½ cup celery, sliced very thin
- ½ small cucumber, peeled and diced
- 1 medium carrot, peeled and grated
- 10 cherry tomatoes, washed, dried, and cut in half
- ½ cup Hellman's® or Best Foods® Mayonnaise
- Salt and freshly-ground pepper to taste
- Dash of garlic salt

DIRECTIONS

1. Cook macaroni according to directions on package.
2. Drain, rinse with cold water, drain again.
3. Sprinkle macaroni with lemon juice, mix well and chill in the fridge for 2 to 3 hours.
4. Add the rest of the ingredients, mix well, and keep refrigerated until ready to serve.

Homemade Potato Salad

Recipe makes 6 servings

Meat and potatoes were the two basic foods when Gramme was growing up, which meant that it was important to know how to make tasty dishes that included potatoes. This was a family favorite and is even better on the second day.

INGREDIENTS

- 2 pounds yellow, red, or white potatoes
- 1 tablespoon lemon juice
- ½ cup sour cream
- ¼ cup Hellman's® or Best Foods® Mayonnaise
- 1 tablespoon prepared yellow mustard
- ½ medium red onion, finely chopped (about ½ cup)
- 3 celery stalks, sliced very thin (about ½ cup)

- 2 hard-boiled eggs, peeled and chopped
- ¼ cup chopped fresh herbs (parsley and/or cilantro)
- Salt and freshly-ground black pepper to taste

DIRECTIONS

1. Scrub the potatoes well, do not peel, and place them in a large pot.
2. Cover with at least 1½ inches of water above potatoes.
3. Season with one tablespoon of salt.
4. Place the pot over medium-high heat and bring to a boil.
5. Reduce heat to low and simmer for 15 to 20 minutes or until potatoes can be easily pierced with a fork.
6. When potatoes are done, drain completely and let cool.
7. Peel potatoes and chop into bite-sized chunks into a large bowl.
8. Sprinkle potatoes with lemon juice and salt.
9. Peel and chop the eggs on top of the potatoes.
10. Add the chopped onions, sliced celery, and herbs to the potatoes.
11. Mix sour cream, mayonnaise, and the mustard in a small bowl.
12. Add sour cream mixture to the potato bowl and gently stir to combine all ingredients. *(Try not to mash the potatoes.)*
13. If needed, add a little extra mayonnaise.
14. Season with salt and pepper to taste.
15. The salad will taste better if you refrigerate at least 30 minutes or more before serving. It allows the flavors to blend.

NOTE: Anything made with mayonnaise must always be kept cold. If it is left sitting out for an extended period, it can go bad.

Sloppy Joes

Recipe makes 8 servings

Our family loves sloppy joes and you can make them easily with this recipe. Have plenty of hamburger buns and napkins ready.

INGREDIENTS

- 1 tablespoon butter
- 1 medium onion, chopped
- 1 clove garlic, minced
- 1 lb. lean ground beef
- 1 (8 ounce) can tomato sauce
- ½ cup ketchup
- 1 tablespoon brown sugar
- 1 teaspoon ground mustard

- 1 tablespoon white vinegar
- 1 tablespoon Worcestershire Sauce
- Salt and freshly-ground black pepper, to taste
- 8 hamburger buns

DIRECTIONS

1. Place one tablespoon butter in a large saucepan or Dutch oven over medium-high heat.
2. Add chopped onion and garlic.
3. Sauté until onion turns transparent and starts to brown.
4. Stir in the ground beef and cook until the meat is crumbly and no longer red, about 5 minutes.
5. Spoon out any excess grease *(with supervision).*
6. In a small bowl, place the tomato sauce, ketchup, brown sugar, mustard, vinegar, Worcestershire Sauce, ¼ teaspoon salt, and 1/8 teaspoon pepper and whisk together until well blended.
7. Pour sauce over beef and stir until meat is evenly-coated.
8. Cover, place over med-low heat and simmer 20 minutes, stirring occasionally.
9. Serve on hamburger buns with sliced onions on the side for people who want them on their sloppy joes.
10. Prepare fresh corn on the cob with butter as the vegetable and a Green Salad.

One Pot Spaghetti

Recipe makes 4 servings

This is one of my favorite recipes because it is so easy to make and cleaning up is simple. For a compete dinner, serve with Green Salad and Garlic Bread!

INGREDIENTS

- 1 tablespoon butter
- 1 medium onion, diced
- 4 cloves garlic, peeled and minced
- 1 lb. lean ground beef
- 3 cup water (or 2¾ cup water and ¼ cup red wine)
- 15 oz. can tomato sauce
- Small can tomato paste
- 15 oz. can diced tomatoes including juice

- 1 tablespoon Italian seasoning
- 1 teaspoon salt
- 1 teaspoon freshly ground black pepper
- ½ teaspoon sugar
- 8 to 10 oz. uncooked spaghetti
- ½ cup freshly grated Parmesan cheese
- 2 tablespoons chopped fresh parsley

DIRECTIONS

1. Place a Dutch oven (or large, heavy-duty sauce pan) over medium-high heat.
2. Place 1 tablespoon butter in the pan, add chopped onion and minced garlic.
3. Sauté until onion becomes transparent and begins to brown.
4. Stir in the ground meat, cook until meat is browned and crumbly.
5. Spoon off any excess fat *(with supervision).*
6. Add water, tomato sauce, tomato paste, diced tomatoes, Italian seasoning, salt, pepper, and sugar.
7. Bring meat sauce to a boil over high heat – then, break spaghetti noodles in half and drop into sauce.
8. Reduce heat to a simmer and cover.
9. Continue cooking, stirring often to be sure noodles are separated.
10. Noodles should be cooked through in 12 to 15 minutes. Add a little water if sauce gets too dry.
11. Stir in the parsley just before removing from heat.
12. Place grated Parmesan Cheese on the table for topping.
13. Serve piping hot with Green Salad.

Garlic Bread

This wonderful garlic bread can be made two different ways – grilled crispy under the boiler (as shown below) or soft and buttery from being wrapped in foil and heated in the oven (picture on following page). Try it both ways and find out which you prefer.

Toasted Deliciousness from the Broiler
(This method requires a lot of supervision!)

INGREDIENTS

- 16-ounce loaf of French bread
- ½ cup (1 stick) unsalted butter, softened
- 1 teaspoon garlic salt
- 1 heaping tablespoon of finely chopped fresh parsley (optional)
- ¼ cup freshly grated Parmesan cheese (optional)

DIRECTIONS

1. Preheat oven to 350° F.
2. Line a heavy-duty cookie sheet with foil.
3. Mix the butter, garlic salt, and parsley together in a small bowl.
4. Cut the loaf of bread in half, lengthwise.
5. Spread a generous amount of the butter mixture over both halves of the bread.
6. Place the bread on the foil-lined cookie sheet and put in the pre-heated oven on the middle rack.
7. Let it heat in the oven for 10 minutes.
8. If you are using Parmesan, remove from the oven and sprinkle with the cheese *(if not using cheese, skip to the next step).*
9. Move the cookie sheet to the highest rack and change the oven to “BROIL” (which is high heat) and broil for 2-3 minutes until the edges of the bread are toasted and the cheese bubbles (if you are using cheese).
10. Watch very carefully while broiling. The bread can quickly go from un-toasted to burnt.
11. Remove from the oven and let bread cool a minute.
12. Cut the halves into 1-inch slices.
13. Serve immediately.

Soft and Buttery from the Oven

(This method needs supervision for cutting and Moving cookie sheet "in and out" of the oven.)

DIRECTIONS

1. Preheat oven to 350° F.
2. Make the butter/garlic/parsley mixture as described above.
3. Cut 1-inch thick slices through the loaf of bread, but do not cut all the way through, cut almost to the bottom crust.
4. Put a teaspoon of the butter mixture between every other slice so that it is only buttered on one side of each slice. If you like super buttery bread put a teaspoon of butter mixture between every slice.
5. Wrap the bread in aluminum foil and heat for 15 minutes in the pre-heated oven.
6. To serve: after it cools a little, cut each slice completely through and place in a covered bread basket.

DESSERTS and SNACKS

All Shook-Up Ice Cream

Recipe is for one serving

This recipe can be a fun activity at a party or family gathering. It is especially good for younger children – although my bet is the entire family will enjoy the fun!

INGREDIENTS (PER SERVING)

- 1 tablespoon sugar
- ½ cup heavy cream
- ¼ teaspoon vanilla
- 6 tablespoons rock salt
- 1 pint-sized Ziploc® plastic bag
- 1 gallon-sized Ziploc® plastic bag
- Plenty of ice

DIRECTIONS

1. Fill the gallon plastic bag half-full of ice and add 6 tablespoons rock salt.
2. Place sugar, cream, and vanilla in the small Ziploc bag and seal it completely (double-check seal).
3. Place the small bag filled with ingredients inside the large bag and seal it completely (double-check seal).
4. Give to one person and instruct him/her to shake until mixture has turned into ice cream, about 6-8 minutes.
5. Remove the small bag from the larger one and rinse.
6. Hand them a spoon, open the bag carefully, and let them enjoy the result of their effort.
7. OPTIONAL: Have fresh fruit (like crushed strawberries) and nuts to add to the finished product.

NOTE: It is a good idea to have the small bags all prepared and in the refrigerator. Also have the ice bags prepared and in the freezer. Then, it will be easy to put them together and pass them out.

Original Toll House® Chocolate Chip Cookies

Recipe makes about 5 dozen cookies

This is the original Toll House® Cookie Recipe from the package. There are dozens of variations you may want to try, but this recipe always works! So, start here and enjoy every scrumptious bite.

INGREDIENTS

- 2¼ cups all-purpose flour
- 1 teaspoon baking soda
- 1 teaspoon salt
- 1 cup (2 sticks) butter, softened
- ¾ cup granulated sugar
- ¾ cup packed brown sugar

- 1 teaspoon vanilla extract
- 2 large eggs
- 2 cups Nestlé® Toll House® Semi-Sweet Chocolate Morsels *(Experiment with Dark Chocolate, White Chocolate, Butterscotch or even a mixture of different flavored morsels)*
- 1 cup chopped nuts (optional)

DIRECTIONS

1. Preheat oven to 375° F.
2. Generously butter two large cookie sheets.
3. Measure and place flour, baking soda, and salt in a small bowl – whisk together; set aside.
4. Place the softened butter, granulated sugar, brown sugar, and vanilla extract in a large mixing bowl and beat with a handheld electric mixer until creamy.
5. Add eggs, one at a time, beating well after each addition.
6. Gradually beat in flour mixture – ½ cup at a time. Beat until well-blended, but don't over mix.
7. Using a wooden spoon, stir in the chocolate morsels and nuts.
8. Use a cookie scoop or a large tablespoon and drop on cookie sheets about 2-3 inches apart.
9. Bake for 9 to 11 minutes or until golden brown.
10. Cool on baking sheets for 2 minutes.
11. Using a pancake turner, remove cookies from pan and let cool on wire racks that have been covered with clean, dry paper towels.
12. Spoon up another batch on the cookie sheets and continue baking until all dough has been used.

COOKING TIPS

- As soon as you remove the cookies from the oven, use two tablespoons to slightly scrunch up the edges. This creates a crispier edge and a softer, chewy center.
- Dough may be stored in refrigerator for up to one week or in freezer for up to eight weeks – and cooked whenever the mood strikes you – one cookie sheet batch at a time.

COOKIE BARS (VARIATION)

1. Preheat oven to 350° F.
2. Butter a 15 X 10-inch jelly-roll pan.
3. Prepare cookie dough exactly as described as above through Step 7.
4. Then, spread the dough into a well-buttered pan and bake for 20 to 25 minutes until golden brown.
5. Set the pan on a wire rack to cool.
6. Cut into squares - Makes 4 dozen bars.

This recipe is from www.VeryBestBaking.com. Nestle® Toll House® is a registered trademark of Société des Produits Nestlé S.A., Vevey, Switzerland.

Easy Chocolate Chip Cookies

Recipe makes 40 cookies

You will love this recipe because it is exactly as the name says: EASY. The cookies can be made in minutes and are the best homemade chocolate chip cookies ever!

INGREDIENTS

- 1 cup melted butter
- 1 cup packed light brown sugar
- ¾ cup granulated sugar
- 2 large eggs
- 2 teaspoons vanilla extract
- 2½ cups flour
- 1 teaspoon baking soda
- ¾ teaspoon salt
- 2 cups (a 12 oz. bag) Ghirardelli® **Grand Semi-sweet** Chocolate Chips

DIRECTIONS

1. Preheat oven to 375° F.
2. In a very large bowl, add the melted butter, brown sugar, and granulated sugar.
3. Whisk until well combined.
4. Add the eggs and vanilla.
5. Whisk until smooth.
6. Add the flour, baking soda, and salt.
7. Stir until well-mixed – be careful not to overmix.
8. Stir in the chocolate chips and continue stirring until chips are completely mixed into the dough.
9. Scoop out 1½ tablespoon-size balls of the batter on a baking sheet, leaving 2 inches between each cookie. (A cookie scoop works well for this.)
10. Bake for 10 to 12 minutes. The center should be soft and the edges should barely be golden. DO NOT OVER BAKE.
11. Cool 3-4 minutes on the cookie sheet.
12. With a pancake turner, carefully move the cookies to a wire rack covered with a clean paper towel.
13. When completely cool, store in a sealable plastic bag.
14. If not eating in the next two or three days, freeze for up to 3 months.
15. Thaw at room temperature, or if in a hurry, microwave for 30 seconds (one at a time).

Chocolate Chip Cookie Cake

Recipe makes 6 servings

A soft, chewy cookie cake filled with chocolate chips and topped with a chocolate buttercream frosting. This is the perfect dessert for a family party or for a sleepover with friends.

INGREDIENTS for the Cookie Cake

- 2 cups all-purpose flour
- ½ teaspoon baking soda
- ¾ teaspoon salt
- 1¾ cup unsalted butter, softened
- ¾ cup light brown sugar, packed
- ¼ cup granulated sugar
- 1 large egg, room temperature
- 1 large egg yolk, room temperature
- 1 teaspoon pure vanilla extract
- 1 cup semi-sweet chocolate chips

INGREDIENTS for the Chocolate Butter Cream Frosting

- ½ cup unsalted butter, softened
- 1½ cups powdered sugar
- ¼ cup unsweetened cocoa powder
- 1 to 2 tablespoons half and half
- ½ teaspoon pure vanilla extract
- Small dash of salt

DIRECTIONS

1. Spray a 9-inch springform pan with nonstick cooking spray or grease with softened butter; set aside.
2. In a large mixing bowl, whisk together the flour, baking soda, and salt; set aside.
3. Place the butter, brown sugar, and granulated sugar in a large mixing bowl.
4. Using a hand-held electric mixer, beat for 1-2 minutes until mixture is well-combined and creamy.
5. Add the egg, egg yolk, and vanilla extract.
6. Continue to beat until ingredients are fully blended.
7. Slowly mix in the dry ingredients and continue mixing until just combined, making sure to stop and scrape down the sides of the bowl with a rubber spatula, as needed. (Don't overmix.)
8. With a wooden spoon, gently mix in the chocolate chips.
9. Scoop the cookie dough into the prepared springform pan and spread it out into one even layer.
10. Bake at 350° F for 25-30 minutes or until the top of the cookie cake is set and lightly browned.
    Note: Cover loosely with foil if needed to prevent excess browning on top of the cookie cake.
11. Remove from the oven, set on a wire rack.
12. Allow to cool completely before removing from the pan.

Make the Frosting

1. In a large mixing bowl using a hand-held electric mixer, beat the softened butter on medium speed for 1-2 minutes or until smooth and fluffy.
2. Add the powdered sugar, scrape down the sides of the bowl, then add the cocoa powder and mix until fully combined.
3. Add the heavy whipping cream, vanilla extract, and salt.
4. Beat on medium speed until fully combined, making sure to scrape down the sides of the bowl with a rubber spatula, as needed.
5. Spread the frosting on the cooled cookie cake,
   (The cake can also be served without the frosting and topped with rich vanilla ice cream.)

RECIPE TIPS

- Store leftover cookie cake in an airtight container at room temperature or in the refrigerator for up to four days.
- Cover cookie cake tightly and store at room temperature for up 2-3 days.
- Cookie cake freezes well for up to 3 months. When ready to serve, thaw overnight in the refrigerator; then, bring to room temperature.
- Make the frosting fresh, no more than a few hours before serving.
- Frosting also freezes well for up to 3 months. Thaw overnight in the refrigerator, bring to room temperature, and mix well before frosting the cookie cake.

Chocolate Mayonnaise Cupcakes

Recipe makes 12 cupcakes

This is a very old family recipe that has been passed down from my Gramme's grandmother. You DO NOT taste the mayonnaise – and it is amazing.

TOOLS

12-cup muffin pan
Cupcake liners
Large and medium-sized mixing bowls
Wire Whisk
Hand-held electric mixer
Rubber spatula
Measuring cups
Measuring spoons

INGREDIENTS

- 2 cups all-purpose (or wheat) flour
- 2/3 cup unsweetened cocoa powder
- 1¼ teaspoons baking soda
- ¼ teaspoon baking powder
- 3 eggs
- 1 2/3 cups sugar
- 1 teaspoon vanilla extract
- 1 cup Hellmann's® or Best Foods® Real Mayonnaise
- 1 1/3 cups water

DIRECTIONS

1. Preheat oven to 350° F.
2. Place one cupcake liner in each well of the cupcake pan; set aside.
3. In medium bowl, combine flour, cocoa, baking soda, and baking powder; set aside.
4. Place eggs, sugar, and vanilla in a large mixing bowl.
5. Beat with hand-held electric mixer set at high speed for 3 minutes or until light and fluffy.
6. Using low speed, beat in Hellmann's® or Best Foods® Real Mayonnaise – mix until well-blended.
7. Alternately beat in flour mixture and water. Begin and end with flour mixture. Be sure to scrap down the sides with a rubber spatula as you mix.
8. Fill each cupcake liner about ¾ full, which will create a nice rounded top on the cupcake.**
9. Bake 30 minutes or until toothpick inserted in center of a cupcake comes out clean.
10. Set on wire rack to cool for 10 minutes.

11. Remove cupcakes from pans and cool completely.
12. Sprinkle with confectioners' sugar or frost with your favorite frosting.

NOTE: My favorite frosting is the next recipe.

***** To BAKE AS A CAKE***

- Prepare batter as directed above and pour into a buttered and lightly-floured 9 X 13-inch baking pan.
- Bake 40 minutes or until toothpick inserted in center comes out clean.
- Remove cake from the oven and set on a wire rack to let it cool completely before frosting.

Vanilla Butter Cream Frosting

Recipe makes about 2 cups frosting – can be doubled easily.

This frosting is perfect for almost any dessert that needs frosting such as: cake, cupcakes, and cookies. Can also be used to "decorate" Christmas Cookies – just add coloring and sprinkles.

INGREDIENTS

- ½ cup butter (1 stick), softened
- 2 cups powdered sugar, sifted
- 1 teaspoons vanilla
- Dash of salt
- 1-2 tablespoons milk, heavy cream, or half-and-half

DIRECTONS

1. Place softened butter into a medium-sized bowl.
2. Beat with electric hand-held mixture set on medium until butter is smooth – about 3 minutes.
3. Add powdered sugar ½ cup at a time; plus, vanilla and dash of salt.
4. After all the sugar has been mixed in, turn the mixer to high speed and beat about 10 seconds to fluff and lighten the frosting.
5. Add milk, heavy cream or half-and-half until the frosting is at spreadable consistency.
6. If you want a stiffer frosting, add more confectioner's sugar, a ¼ cup at a time.
7. If you want softer frosting, add more milk or cream, a tablespoon at a time.

NOTE: To make chocolate frosting, add 1/3 cup unsweetened cocoa as you are mixing in the powdered sugar. (Powdered sugar is also known as Confectioners' Sugar)

Banana Chocolate Chip Energy Bites

Recipe makes 20 bites

INGREDIENTS

- 1¼ cup rolled oats
- 1 tablespoon chia seeds or wheat germ
- ⅓ cup maple syrup
- ¼ cup almond butter
- 1 ripe banana, mashed
- 1 teaspoon pure vanilla extract
- 1 teaspoon ground cinnamon
- ¼ cup semi-sweet chocolate chips

DIRECTIONS

1. Mix all ingredients in a medium to large bowl.
2. Cover the bowl and let the batter sit in the fridge at least three hours or overnight. 2-3 The batter will be sticky; but, it will firm up as it sits.
3. With damp hands press the mixture into 20 energy balls.
4. Cover lightly with wax paper and place the prepared energy balls in the fridge for at least two hours – preferably overnight. They will become firm as they chill.
5. Great for breakfast, a quick snack, or as a healthy treat in lunch boxes.
6. Refrigerate for up to 5-6 days – or freeze up to three months. Best if the bites thaw at room temperature for 20 minutes before eating.

Creamy Chocolate Nut Fudge

Recipe makes 36 1-inch pieces

This creamy, nutty chocolate fudge can be made in less than 10 minutes. Your family and friends will think you are an amazing cook.

INGREDIENTS

- 2 cups dark chocolate chips (12 oz bag)
- 1 can (14 ounces) sweetened condensed milk
- ¼ cup butter
- 1 teaspoon vanilla extract
- 1 cup chopped pecans plus about 2 tablespoons for topping

DIRECTIONS

1. Butter the bottom of a square baking pan or line it with parchment paper.
2. In a medium-sized glass mixing bowl, mix together the chocolate chips, condensed milk, and butter.
3. Heat in the microwave for 90 seconds.
4. Stir the mixture to blend and heat another 25 seconds if chips are not all melted.
5. Add the vanilla extract and stir until smooth.
6. Add the chopped pecans (optional).
7. Scoop the chocolate mixture into the prepared pan and spread evenly with a rubber spatula.
8. Top with remaining 2 tablespoons chopped pecans (optional).
9. Let the fudge harden – you may need to place in the fridge for 30 minutes or longer.

10. Cut into 1-inch squares and store in an airtight container in the fridge for a week.
11. Enjoy this delicious treat with friends and family!

Note:

- *Nuts are optional. Many people prefer their fudge plain.*
- *If you prefer, instead of using the microwave you can melt the chocolate, milk and butter in a double boiler on the top of the stove – (May need supervision.)*

Chocolate Peanut Butter Fudge

Recipe makes 30 pieces

Chocolate and peanut butter – is there any combination better than that? This recipe creates two melt-in-your-mouth layers of deliciousness - chocolate fudge layered on top of peanut butter fudge. Made in the microwave – so quick and easy, you will be blown away.

INGREDIENTS

- 1 cup Laura Scudders© Natural SMOOTH Peanut Butter (brand makes a difference)
- 1 cup butter
- 2 teaspoons vanilla divided
- 3½ cups powdered sugar (measure carefully)
- Dash of salt
- 1 small can (7 oz) sweetened condensed milk
- 1½ cups semisweet chocolate chips (12 oz bag is TWO cups)
- 2 tablespoons butter

DIRECTIONS

Make the Peanut Butter Fudge

1. Place the peanut butter and butter in a large microwave safe bowl.
2. Microwave for 1 minute and 30 seconds.
3. Stir well and return to the microwave for another one minute and 30 seconds.
4. When mixture is blended, add salt and one teaspoon of vanilla.
5. Add the powdered sugar one cup at a time, mixing well after each addition. (Mixture will be very thick.)
6. Spread into a buttered 9 X 13 baking dish – if you like thicker pieces, use a square baking dish instead.
7. Cover with plastic wrap, and chill in the refrigerator for at least 30 minutes.

After Chilling . . . **Make the Chocolate Fudge**

8. Place the sweetened condensed milk, chocolate chips, and butter in a microwave safe bowl,
9. Microwave for one minute – remove from microwave and stir to blend the ingredients.
10. Continue microwaving and stirring in 30 second bursts until mixture is completely melted and smooth.
11. Stir in the remaining one teaspoon vanilla.
12. Add ½ cup of nuts (optional).
13. Spread the chocolate fudge over the peanut butter fudge.
14. Return to the refrigerator for at least 2 hours – or until set.
15. Cut into 30 pieces.

This is so delicious, it may disappear before it has time to chill completely!

Libby's® Pumpkin Pie

Recipe makes eight servings

Gramme says she has tried many pumpkin pie recipes and this is by far the easiest and the best pumpkin pie of all – so, she says, "Why mess with success?"

INGREDIENTS

- ¾ cup granulated sugar
- 1 teaspoon ground cinnamon
- ½ teaspoon salt
- ½ teaspoon ground ginger
- ¼ teaspoon ground cloves
- 2 large cage-free eggs
- 1 can (15 oz.) LIBBY'S® 100% Pure Pumpkin
- 1 can (12 oz.) evaporated milk

- 1 unbaked 9-inch Pillsbury™ Refrigerated Pie Crust
- Freshly whipped cream – lightly sweetened

DIRECTIONS

1. Pre-heat the oven to 425° F.
2. Follow the directions on the Pillsbury™ Refrigerated Pie Crust to prepare one 9-inch pie crust.
3. Crimp the edges of the crust and set aside.
4. In a small bowl, mix together the sugar, cinnamon, salt, ginger and cloves using a wire whisk to stir.
5. Place the eggs in a large bowl and beat until fluffy.
6. Stir in pumpkin and sugar-spice mixture.
7. Mix all the ingredients until well-blended.
8. Gradually stir in evaporated milk – continue stirring until mixture is smooth and creamy.
9. Pour into prepared pie shell.
10. Place a pie-crust protector on the pie.
11. Bake in preheated 425°F oven for 15 minutes.
12. Reduce heat to 350°F and continue baking for 40 to 50 minutes or until a knife inserted near the center of the pie comes out clean.
13. Cool on a wire rack for at least 2 hours.
14. Serve immediately or refrigerate.
15. Top each piece with whipped cream before serving.

Note: Please ask for help when placing the pie in the oven and removing it – just to be safe.

Pumpkin Pie Cobbler

Recipe makes 12 servings

If you are not quite ready to make a pumpkin pie, this is an easy, delicious alternative. You can put It together in 20 minutes or less, cook for 45 minutes and you are finished.

INGREDIENTS

- Soft butter, for greasing the pan
- 1 package Pillsbury™ Refrigerated Pie Crust Mix
- 6 large cage-free eggs
- 1 cup granulated sugar
- ½ cup light brown sugar (packed)
- 1 cup heavy cream
- 2 (15 oz) cans pumpkin puree
- 2 teaspoons vanilla
- 1 tablespoon ground cinnamon
- 2 teaspoons ground ginger
- 1 teaspoon ground allspice
- ½ teaspoon ground nutmeg
- ½ teaspoon salt
- Turbinado sugar (for sprinkling the top)

DIRECTIONS

1. Preheat the oven to 375° F.
2. Lightly butter a 9 x 13-inch pan.
3. Open the package and roll out the Pillsbury™ Pie Crust onto a large cookie sheet covered with parchment paper.
4. Cut the dough into random shapes with a knife or pastry cutter.

5. Cover the pan loosely with plastic wrap, and refrigerate while you complete the next step

Make the Custard

6. In a medium bowl, whisk the eggs, sugar, and brown sugar to combine.
7. Whisk in the heavy cream, then add the pumpkin puree and vanilla extract.
8. Add the cinnamon, ginger, allspice, nutmeg, and salt - whisk to combine.
9. Pour the custard into the buttered baking dish.

Add the Pie Crust Pieces and Bake

10. Lay the chilled pie dough strips on top of the custard, overlapping slightly as needed.
11. ***Egg wash**** the surface of the pie dough and sprinkle the top evenly with turbinado sugar.
12. Bake, 40-45 minutes or until crust is a deep golden brown.
13. Serve warm or cool with whipped cream.

* ***Egg Wash*** is made with one egg (white, whole, or yolk) beaten with 1 tablespoon of water, milk or cream. It makes the pastry shine and bakes to a golden brown.

To Prepare the Egg Wash:

Whip the egg and liquid together in a small bowl until well combined and apply with a pastry brush.

No-bake Chocolate Peanut Butter Oatmeal Cookies

Recipe makes 24 cookies

These are simple and fun to make. A perfect first-time cooking experience *(supervision recommended).*

INGREDIENTS

- ½ cup butter, softened
- 2 cups granulated sugar
- ½ cup milk
- 4 tablespoons unsweetened cocoa
- ½ cup creamy natural peanut butter (well stirred – be sure no excess oil remains)
- 2 teaspoons vanilla extract (OR - ½ teaspoon almond extract with 1½ teaspoons vanilla)
- 3 cups quick oats (not old-fashioned)

DIRECTIONS

1. Mix the butter, sugar, milk and cocoa in a large sauce pan.
2. Bring to a rolling boil, stirring continuously for 1 minute.
3. Remove from heat.
4. Add peanut butter to the hot mixture and stir until melted.
5. Add vanilla extract (or almond/vanilla extract blend).
6. Stir in the oats until well blended.
7. Drop 1 tablespoon at a time onto wax paper.
8. Let cool until set.

Protein Energy Bites

Recipe makes 24 Energy Bites

Easy, no-bake, healthy, energy-filled snacks, made with all-natural ingredients. Perfect for school lunches. Place frozen bites in a plastic bag. They will thaw and be ready to eat by lunchtime.

TOOLS

Mini-muffin pan
Large mixing bowl
Sturdy wooden spoon

INGREDIENTS (BASIC RECIPE)

- Softened butter
- ½ cup pure peanut butter
- 1 cup old-fashioned oats
- 1 cup chopped raw almonds/pecans/walnuts (your choice)
- ¼ cup organic honey
- ¼ cup chocolate chips (optional)

DIRECTIONS

1. Lightly butter each mini-muffin well.
2. Stir all ingredients together in a large bowl with a sturdy wooden spoon.
3. Mix until well blended.
4. Refrigerate for at least one hour.
5. Use a cookie scoop or tablespoon to place mixture into each mini-muffin well.

6. Freeze for at least three hours.
7. Remove from pan.
   NOTE: If the energy bites stick to the pan, set the pan in warm water for one minute.
8. Thaw and serve.
   NOTE: The bites can be stored in the fridge up to one week or frozen for up to 2 months.

CHANGE-UP THE RECIPE FOR FUN!

- Replace peanut butter with almond butter.
- Use ¾ cup dried blueberries, cranberries, or cherries mixed with ½ cup sliced almonds and a dash of cinnamon instead of nuts only.
- Use 1/3 cup dried cherries, 1/3 cup chocolate chips, and 1/3 cup chopped pecans with 1 tablespoon cocoa powder.
- Use ¼ cup almond butter instead of peanut butter with 1 cup chopped walnuts, 1/3 cup chopped pitted dates and ¼ to 1/3 cup maple syrup instead of honey.

World's Best Cheesecake

Recipe makes 8 servings

This one of my family's favorite desserts - always part of holiday meals and most birthdays. It is also extremely easy to make. Serve plain with little fruit garnish on top; with crushed, lightly-sweetened strawberries; or drizzle with chocolate. Be creative!

INGREDIENTS

CRUST

- 18 graham crackers, crushed.
- 6 tablespoons butter (no substitutes)
- ¼ cup sugar

CREAM CHEESE FILLING

- 4 three-ounce packages cream cheese, room temperature
- ½ cup sugar

- 2 large eggs
- ½ lemon (juice only) – hand squeezed

SOUR CREAM TOPPING

- ½ pint cup sour cream (1 cup)
- 1 tablespoon sugar
- ½ teaspoon vanilla extract

DIRECTIONS

Make the Crust

1. Pre-heat the oven to 350° F.
2. Melt butter in the microwave; set aside.
3. Place crackers in a heavy plastic bag and roll with a rolling pin until finely crushed. (This should be done in small batches).
4. Place 1½ cups of the graham crackers crumbs in a medium-sized bowl.
5. Add sugar and mix thoroughly.
6. Stir in the melted butter and mix until well-blended.
7. Press the mixture into a 9" pin plate.
8. Bake for 8 to 10 minutes – let cool while mixing the filling.

Alternate Crust

- Use a packaged prepared graham cracker crust and bake in hot oven (400° F.) for 5 minutes – set aside to cool.
- This crust works, but. it is not as tasty as the homemade version above.

Make the Cream Cheese Filling

1. With a hand electric mixer, blend the following: cream cheese, sugar, eggs, lemon juice. Mix until smooth.
2. Pour into graham cracker crust.
3. Bake for 25 - 30 minutes – center should be a little soft (DO NOT OVERCOOK).
4. Cool at least 15 minutes on wire rack before adding sour cream topping.

Make the Sour Cream Topping

1. Increase the oven temperature to 400° F.
2. Add 1 tablespoon sugar and ½ teaspoon vanilla to the sour cream and mix well.
3. Spread the topping carefully cover the cream cheese pie. Be sure the topping touches the edges of the crust.
4. Bake 5 to 7 minutes (do not overcook).
5. Cool on wire rack.
6. It is best to refrigerate overnight before serving.

About the Author

Nancy N Wilson, an Arizona native, has enjoyed tremendous opportunities both personally and professionally.

She has lived and worked on both the East Coast and West Coast of the United States; consulted with major corporations in Europe and Japan; and traveled extensively throughout Central and South America.

In 2007, she returned to Arizona to live near her two sons and to do what she has always wanted to do – WRITE.

Her primary goal was to become a published author. That dream was first realized in 2012 and continues to this day.

This is her "Lucky 13" cookbook and there are two more cookbooks to be published soon.

Her first cookbooks, the complete *Mama's Legacy Series,* are listed on the following page, plus other cookbooks she has written. The list includes two very popular "must haves": *Candy Making Made Easy* and *Cake Making Made Easy.*

All her books can be purchased as eBooks or in paperback through Amazon.com through a single click on each of the links provided.

Pick-up your copies today!

Other Books by Nancy N. Wilson

Cookbooks

Candy Making Made Easy - Instructions and 17 Starter Recipes

Cake Making Made Easy - Instructions and 60 Cakes

Cook Ahead – Freezer to Table

The Healthy Diet Cookbook

Garden Fresh Soups and Stews

Sweet Treats

Single, On-You-Own, and Hungry

Mama's Legacy Cookbooks Series

Seven Volumes Available

Dinner – 55 Easy Recipes (Volume I)

Breakfast and Brunch – 60 Delicious Recipes (Volume II)

Dessert – 50 Scrumptious Choices (Volume III)

Chicken – 25 Classic Dinners (Volume IV)

Mexican Favorites – 21 Traditional Recipes (Volume V)

Side Dish Recipes (Volume VI)

Sauce Recipes – 50 Tasty Choices (Volume VII)

Health and Fitness

DETOX – The Master Cleanse Diet

Growing Tomatoes

Juicing for Life

Stop Eating Yourself into an Early Grave

The Secret to Successful Dieting

Wow! You Look Fantastic!

Business

Attitude Adjustment

Navigating the Internet Jungle

Congratulations! You Are Self-Employed

Books Written Under Pen Names

Everything You Need to Know About Growing Roses (Sumner)

Power Up Your Brain - Five Simple Strategies (Jackson)

Clicker Training for Dogs (Ellsworth)

Making Money with Storage Unit Auctions (Cranston)

All books can be purchased through Amazon.com.

They are available as eBooks and as paperbacks.

Made in the USA
Monee, IL
26 October 2022